TURNING YOUR DOWNFALLS INTO SUCCESS

TANIESHA RAMSEY-LANE

TRANSFORMING YOUR DOWNFALLS INTO YOUR SUCCESS.

Being Successful Is In Our Veins Everyone Has That Drive Inside Of Them. You Just Have To Dig Deep Down Inside Of Your Soul And Find It. Bring It Out To Reality. Your Purpose On God's Green Earth Is To Dream And Vision. We Are Put On This Earth To Be Successful. We Have The 5 Sense Of Success.

1. Plan
2. Review
3. Action
4. Success
5. The Success Cycle

Plan: This Is Where We Plan What We're Going To Achieve. When And How.

Review: Here We Review How You're Progressing Compared To Your Plan.

Action: Then We Brainstorm Ideas And Proactive Action Points To Keep You On Track With Your Plan.

Success: This Is Were You Enjoy The Results Increased Growth, Increased Profitability And Improve Cashflow.

The Success Cycle: A Proven Plan To Help Your Business Grow.

You Will Feel Pain

Every Successful Person Travels A Painful Journey. You Will Want To Give Up Prematurely. Do You Ever Feel Tempted To Give Up? We All Strive For Success. While It Is Encouraging To Think About Reaching Your Goals. Most People Don't Want To Hear About Or Experience The Pain It Takes To Become Successful. Nobody Is Successful . We Have To Work Hard For What We Have Now. Working Hard And Experiencing Pain Is Necessary To Grow, Achieve And Thrive.

How Do You Think You Will Be Able To Handle Newfound Success If Your Character And Personality Are Not Shape And Sharpened By Trail? You Are Going To Have To Know How To Handle And Deal With Pressure. Because Life Throws Both The Positive And Negative At You.

It's Important To Learn How To Cope With Both of Them. While The Pain Of Success Is Undoubtedly Important Along Your Journey It Can Also Be Very Slow- Paced. Because Moving Day By Day Can Be Especially Challenging.

Perhaps Right Now You Feel Overlooked, Forgotten, Mistreated, And You Want To Quit.

Satan's Goal Is To Get You To Do Just That Throw In The Towel And Call It's Quits. Discouragement Is His Favorite Weapon

But Remember This: While Disappointments Are Inevitable, Discouragement Is A Choice.

God Often Uses Trail To Position Us For Greater Blessings. Even In Times Of Great Disappointment, He Knows How He Wants To Use The Disappointment Or Hardship For Our Benefit, And He Desires That We See Him As Our Only Source Of Salvation And Blessings.

You Will Wonder What Direction Do I Go

As You Wonder Through Your More Directionless Time On Your Journey You Will Experience Intense Movement Of Feeling Lost And Hopeless.

If You Are In An Emotionally Or Physically Difficult Spot Right Now, Refuse To Become Discouraged. Ask The Lord To Reveal His Will And Plan For Your Life. Commit Yourself To Him And Pray To Obey No Matter What It Costs.

If You Take This Approach, Then God Will Provide For You In Ways That Far Exceed Human Understanding. You Were Born With These Unique Qualities And You Are Well Equipped To Accomplish That Phenomenal Thing You Were Born To Do. So Just Push Forward And Accomplish All Goals.

You Will Lose Relationships

As You Succeed There Will Be A Handful Of People Who Will Not Be Willing To Support You. That's Fine Don't Let It Discourage You. Remember Everyone Is Not Your Customers And Everyone Won't Make It To The Top With You . You Should Always Be Your #1 Supporter.

As You Be More Successful Your Circle In Life Will Change. For The Good And The Bad . But It Will Be For The Best. You Will Live And Learn Through Life Lessons. Stay Focused On The Prize. Knock All Your Goals One By One . Get Your Mindset Right Remember You Are Not Average. Brand Yourself Speak With Confidence. Don't Paralyze Yourself From Your Business. Remember, This Quote.

If It's Not Making Me Money

Making Me Better , Or Making Me Happy I'm Not Making Time For It. Success Take A Tremendous Amount Of Effort And Sacrifice.

People Will Discourage You

There Is A Popular Thought That You Should Keep Your Dreams Close To Your Chest. Because If You Share Them You May Pillage Them To Dream-Stealers. The Human Mind Is Programmed To Believe The Negative. Work Quite And Let Your Success Do The Work.

You Can't Stop People From Acting Badly Or Letting You Down But You Don't Have To Let It Derail You From Living A Happy And Successful Life.

These Strategies Can Help You Recover From Your Hurt And Anger And Move Forward With Confidence.

1. Allow Your Feelings Being Rejected, Let Down, Or Betrayed.
2. Acknowledge You Unmeet Needs Think About What Needs Of Yours Are

Not Being Met By This Person's Response.

3. Take Care Of Yourself Are There Ways You Can Meet The Unmeet Need For Yourself? The Important Thing Is Not To Give Up And Stew In Passive Resentment. It May Help To Write Down Your Feelings And Try To Give Yourself Compassion, Rather Than Exacerbating The Hurt By Being Self-Critical When Others Behave Badly.

4. Decide If You Need To Speak Up Think About whether It Would Be Productive To Speak Up About Your Feelings Of Disappointment or Betrayal.

5. Examine Your Expectations Think About Whether Your Expectations Are Reasonable In This Situation, And Whether The Person Is Capable Of Doing What you Expect.

6. Set Boundaries If You Need To. If This Person Has A Pattern Of Disappointing Or Betraying You , Think About What You Need To Do To Protect Yourself. Boundaries Can Help You Feel Emotionally Safe. And They Help Restore Your Self-Worth And Self-Respect.

You Will Be Hated For No Reason

There Is A Jealousy That Comes Along With Being Different, Standing Out And Humbly Chasing Your Dreams Small People Envy These Who Have Or Do Everything They Lack.

Reality Is, People Don't Tend To Like Other Successful People. Don't Let There Hate Stop You From Being Great. Pray For Your Haters And Push Through And Focus.

Never Waste Your Time Thinking About People Who Envy , Hate You And Try To Bring You Down Just Because You Succeed Where They Fail. Focus On Those Who Love, Support And Cherish You For Who You Truly Are.

You Will Doubt Yourself

When You Start A New Venture You Will Go In And Out Of Feeling Paralyzed That You Can't Do This " There Is No Fear In Love".

When You Feel Gripped By Fear Turn And Gaze Upon God, Redirect Your Heart To Love Speak To Your Fear. Believe In Yourself. Never Let A Stumble In Your Road Be The End Of Your Journey.

- Forget Failure
- Forget Mistake
- Forget Everything Except What You're Going To Do Now.

And Do It!

You Will Fail

Risk Taking Is At The Very Heart Of Any Quest For Success. You Must Avoid Of The Unknown And See What Happens. When Striving For Success You Will Consistently Face Choices Which Involve Risk. Risk Is, By Nature, Scary. You May Lose Your Lie Savings Or Lose Your Reputation You will Likely Have To Pick Up The Pieces And Start Over Again Time And Again. On Any Path Towards Success You Give Up What You Know For What Could Be. Hope is Your Dope And Putting God First And Prayer In Everything You Do. Failure's Purpose Is To Tune Your Effort Towards Success. Gain Much Knowledge As Possible It's Very Important For Business Owners. You Must Not Stop Learning As Learning

Inspires Your Growth . You Must Fuel Your Creativity Constantly To Reach Your Full Potential. You Already Have All You Need To Succeed. Believe It By Faith.

As An Aspiring Entrepreneur, You Have Probably Face Amount Of Doubt.

You Begin To Wonder If You Are Really Good Enough, If you Can Really Achieve Your Goals, And If You Will Ever Find Real Success In Your Career. While These Feelings May Be Discouraging, The Good News Is That As An Inspiring Entrepreneur , You Are Not Alone. Many Others In Your Position Are Also Dealing With That Has Been Term " Imposter Syndrome". Imposter Syndrome Encompasses A Wide Range Of Feelings.

It Includes Worrying That You're Aren't Smart Enough, Talented Enough, Or Good

Enough To Achieve Your Dreams. Sometimes People Begin To Think That It Was Luck, Not Skill, That Helped Them To Achieve Success. While Some People Allow Imposter Syndrome To Discourage Them From Achieving Their Dreams, It Can Also Encourage People To Work Harder , Helping Them To Prove To Themselves As Well As Others That They Can Achieve Their Dreams.

Even The Most Successful People Deal With It

When You Are Dealing With Imposter Syndrome, You May Begin To Feel Like No One Has Felt The Way You Feel.

You Might Start To Feel That Everyone Else Is Confident And Like You Are, The Only One Simply Pretending To Feel Confident

The Negativity Of It

Unfortunately, If You Allow The Negative Feelings To Take Over, Imposter Syndrome Can Destroy You A First-Time Entrepreneur. Because The Doubt Themselves, They Fail To Try Their Hardest. Sometime They Think If They Stay In The Shadows, Not Standing Out Too Much, Others Will Not Realize They Are Actually A Fraud. They May Also Talk Themselves Out Of Doing Something They Really Want To Do, Convincing Themselves That They'll Just Fail Anyway.

This Lack Of Confidence In Themselves And Their Reluctance to Take Chances May Prevent The Person From Achieving Entrepreneurial Success.

See The Good In Imposter Syndrome

One Important Key To Moving From An Aspiring Entrepreneur To A Successful Entrepreneur Is To Use Imposter Syndrome To Your Advantage. While It Can Bring You Down , Discouraging You, And Preventing You From Achieving Your Goals, It Can Also Be A Great Thing.

Realizing That You Are Not Perfect And That you Need To work Harder To Be Your Best Could Help You To Become Your Best. One Way To See The Good In Imposter Syndrome Is To Talk About It With Others Who May Be Facing The Same Feelings. While Many Entrepreneurs Are Reluctant To Admit That To Admit That They Doubt Their

Own Abilities Admitting It Can Help Others, Who May Feel The Same Way.

Imposter Syndrome May Also Help You To Be More Careful. Double-Checking Yourself And Thinking Through An Idea Will Help You Avoid Blind Confidence.

In The End , Allowing Yourself To Fail Sometimes And Accepting That Entrepreneurial Success May Take Time Will Help You Fight Imposter Syndrome.

When You Are Feeling Down On Yourself, Remember To Focus On Your Successes Feel Small. Remember, Keep The Mind Sharp, The Vision Clear, Resolve Strong And You Will Make It!

It Will All Be Worth It

To Achieve Anything You Have To Think Positive About What You Are Doing. You Have To Believe You Will Succeed, And You Have To Trust In God And The Process. The Vision Is The Prize. Not The Money Or The End Result. To Have An Impact, To Make A Difference? You Can Only Know Your Impact You Have Upon Others. When You See That Your Success Improves And Positively Influences The Lives Of Others, It Will Be Worth It. I Don't Believe Designation To Be A Place. I Believe Designation To Be A Feeling. It Is A Experience To Deeply Move And Contribute To The World At Large. The Type Of Designation Makes The Struggle Of The Journey Well Worth It.

Put Yourself On The Road To Success With These 5 Principles

Depending On Whom You Ask Success Means Different Things. If You Were To Ask Me, I'd Say It Means Having A Career That Revolves Around Real Life. The First Step In Achieving Success Is Often Deciding What It Means To You.

Chances Are Your Answers Similar to Mine. But Whatever Your Version Of Success, People Who Want To Be Successful Should Mimic The Behaviors Of The Great Ones Who Came Before Them.

These Behavior Includes:

- Follow Your Talent: It's Helpful To Be Passionate About Your Pursuits, But Passion Without Talent Is Like A Car Without A Full Tank Of Gas. It Won't Get You Know As Far As You Want To Go. Everyone Has A Gift, So Find Yours And Put In The Time To Make Yourself Better At It.
- Focus Your Quest: So The Road To Success For Some Can Be This Simple
- Focus Your Quest On One Big Goal, And Remember That A Jack-Of-All-Trades Is Usually A Master Of None.
- Limit Your Option: Keep Your Options Open Almost Seems To Be Our Country's Motto. Our Affinity For Keeping Options Open Unfortunately Leads Us To Limit Ourselves Because It Paves The Road To Mediocrity, Rather Than One To Success. By

Limiting Your Options You Go All In, And Force Yourself To Give Your Utmost Effort To Achieve A Goal. However, Making A Commitment To The One Path Or Goal Can Also Lead You To Try Harder And Potentially Be More Successful In Your Efforts.

- Work Towards Meaningful Goals: Most People Are Obsessed With Efficiency, Which Leads Them To Work Towards Goals That Are Meaningless, Empty Or Simply Unimportant . Effectiveness On The Other Hand, Is Not About Getting As Much Done As Possible In A Limited Amount Of Time Rather, It's About Getting Things Accomplished That Matter.
- Never Give Up: But If You Have A Goal That Is Achievable Through Actual

Talent And Hard Work , Don't Give Up Ever. You Will Make Mistakes, And You Will Fail. So Keep Practicing, Learning, Accepting Rejection And Trying Again. The Road To Success Is Always Under Construction.

Success Comes To Those Who Keep Going. As Long As You're Moving Towards Your Dream Goals, You're Winning. Keep Going.

Consistency- One Of The Issues That I Often See When It Comes To Entrepreneurialism Is Consistency. Most Entrepreneurs Are Inconsistent. The One Thing I Tell Them To Do Simple: Create A Schedule And Stick To It Daily. Sounds Easy But Is Mostly Challenging.

Stay Consistent With Your Actions. Keep Things Simple. A Schedule As An Entrepreneur Is Your Routine. Your Routine Builds Confidence. Confidence Comes From Repetition, Consistency And The Ability To Predict An Outcome.

Ego And Pride

These Two Mental Blocks Stop Most People From Making Any Progress In Their Business As An Entrepreneur.

Ego Is The Killer To Reality. As An Entrepreneur You'll Naturally Have An Ego. Especially When You See Results From What You 're Doing. The Key Is Being Consciously Aware Of What You're Doing When It Comes To Being Objective About The Results That Are Produced In Relation To The Output Of Work. In Other Words, Trust The Process And The Work Over Your Own Ego. It's Nothing Wrong To Have An Ego. We All Have An Ego, The Most Important Thing Is To Not Allow The Ego To Take Over And Make Decisions For You. Keep Your Ego In Check. Make Daily Check Ins With Yourself When It Comes To Being Accountable For Your Actions. Don't Allow Your Ego To Get In The Way Of The

Of The Facts And Numbers. Pride Can Stall Progress. Pride Doesn't Allow You To Open Your Mindset To Learn New Things. There Is A Reason That Pride Comes Before The Fall. It's Just A Matter Of What Kind Of Mindset Do You Have. The Best Way To Keep Yourself From, Allowing These Two Demons To Ruin Your Life When It Comes To Being A Beast As An Entrepreneur Is To Be Painfully Accountable.

When You're Painfully Accountable To Your Actions. You Have A Mindset That Every Action Means Something. You Don't Waste Time With Anything Outside Of The Data Collected On Your Actions. You Take Control Of Your Own Fate. You Don't Expect Praise. Don't Allow Yourself To Let Ego And Pride Become The Downfall Of Your Business. Keep Your Mindset Sharp And Be Consciously Aware Of The Actions You Take By Remaining Painfully Accountable

To Yourself. You Owe It To Yourself To Become Super Successful.

The Questions That Need Answering On A Daily Basis Are These:

- What's The Purpose Of My Entrepreneurial Journey? (Find Your Why)
- What Problem Am I Looking To Solve?
- Have I Figured Out How To Acquire Customers And How To Retain Them?
- Have I Reached Up And Reached Out To The Right People?

Have I Gone All-in Everyday With The Mindset That I Will Become Successful And Have My Actions Been In Line With That Mindset Everyday?

Success Isn't Easy. It's Challenging. Most People Think Success In Business Is Something That Happens In 6-12 Months. Can It Happen? Of Course. Does It Generally Happen? No. In Fact, Most Businesses Take Years To Get To A Point Where Things Are Running Smoothly And The Business Is Turning Profit. Every Successful Entrepreneur Started Somewhere.

There's No "Majic Pill" That Effortlessly Launches You Out Of Your Cubicle Confinement And Into The Free World Of Entrepreneurship. For Some, The Dream To Be Your Own Boss Grows For A Long Time, Even Years, Before It Finally Comes To Fruition.

The Truth Is, Greater Success In Business Grows From Just One Tiny Seed.

After The Fear And Hurdles I Came Very Close To Failure. Instead Of Giving Up, I Started To Develop A Deep Sense Of Passion For

Motivating And Educating Myself To Reach Greater Heights In Business And Income. It Became A Challenge For Me.

My Desire To Build, Create, And Learn Surpass My Fears. Become A Greater Experience Of Learning My True Power.

Who Am I

I Am A Black African American Woman, Entrepreneur That's Striving For Success. My Name Is Taniesha Ramsey-Lane I Was Born In Dunkirk, New York October 11,1979. I Am 38 Years Old . I Am Married To A Amazing Man Name Ensewell Lane We Have 4 Adorable Kids , Malik 11, Samari 9, Shaniya 6, And Jalen 2. My Lovely Parents Are Mary Thomas-Trotter And Robert Ramsey. Growing Up I Was Blessed To Have Parents That Was Able To Provide The Best Things In Life For Me.

I Went To The Best Schools Had Amazing Teachers. I Was Always A Honor Roll Student. I Always Knew I Wanted To Be A Entrepreneur . To Be Remember As A Legend . To Lead By Example , To Provide

For My Kids So They Wouldn't Have To Worry About Struggling. But Coming Up I Did Deal With Some Struggles In Life. Loss Love Ones And Friends That Inspired Me To Do Better In Life. I Will Never Forget What They Have Taught Me, The Knowledge That They Shared With Me. And Remember Successful Quotes That They Told Me. I Am A Rape Victim That Over Came Hurt And Pain On Many Occasions. I Know How It Feels To Lose Everything And To Bounce Back Up. God Has Bless Me With My Life 4 Times I Skipped Death. I Am Truly Blessed And Highly Favored. I Have A Skills Background in Life Insurance, Retail Sales, Administrator Assistant, Data Entry, Accountant, Office Professional, Medical Billing And Coding, Professional Cosmetologist, And Financial Advisor. I

Own 2 Businesses, Trixxie's House Of Styles And Marvelous Credit. I Enjoy Helping People , Either Helping Them Look Celebrity Famous Or Helping Them Get Out Of Debt, And Having Financial Freedom. Hopefully This First Book Help Someone To Focus On There Why And What And Who Are They Doing It For. Never Give Up , Go Hard, Keep Your Eyes On The Prize, Success Doesn't Happen Over Night , But If You Keep Pushing And Stay Strong You Will Succeed With God's Help.

www.ingramcontent.com/pod-product-compliance
Lightning Source LLC
Chambersburg PA
CBHW031559210526
45464CB00003B/1347